The Growing Up Book for Boys

by the same author

The Growing Up Guide for Girls
What Girls on the Autism Spectrum Need to Know!
Davida Hartman
Illustrated by Margaret Anne Suggs
ISBN 978 1 84905 574 1
eISBN 978 1 78450 038 2

Sexuality and Relationship Education for Children and Adolescents with Autism Spectrum Disorders
A Professional's Guide to Understanding, Preventing Issues, Supporting Sexuality and Responding to Inappropriate Behaviours
Davida Hartman
Illustrated by Kate Brangan
ISBN 978 1 84905 385 3
eISBN 978 0 85700 755 1

of related interest

Making Sense of Sex
A Forthright Guide to Puberty, Sex and Relationships for People with Asperger's Syndrome
Sarah Attwood
Illustrated by Jonathon Powell
ISBN 978 1 84310 374 5
eISBN 978 1 84642 797 8

Personal Hygiene? What's that Got to Do with Me?
Pat Crissey
Illustrated by Noah Crissey
ISBN 978 1 84310 796 5
eISBN 978 1 84642 114 3

The Asperkid's (Secret) Book of Social Rules
The Handbook of Not-So-Obvious Social Guidelines for Tweens and Teens with Asperger Syndrome
Jennifer Cook O'Toole
Illustrated by Brian Bojanowski
ISBN 978 1 84905 915 2
eISBN 978 0 85700 685 1

The
Growing Up
BOOK *for*
BOYS

What Boys on the Autism Spectrum Need to Know!

DAVIDA HARTMAN

Illustrated by MARGARET ANNE SUGGS

Jessica Kingsley *Publishers*
London and Philadelphia

First published in 2015
by Jessica Kingsley Publishers
73 Collier Street
London N1 9BE, UK
and
400 Market Street, Suite 400
Philadelphia, PA 19106, USA

www.jkp.com

Library of Congress Cataloging in Publication Data
A CIP catalog record for this book is available from the Library of Congress

British Library Cataloguing in Publication Data
A CIP catalogue record for this book is available from the British Library

ISBN 978 1 84905 575 8
eISBN 978 1 78450 039 9

Printed and bound in China

CONTENTS

Dedicated to all the strong, handsome and able boys on the autism spectrum in the sometimes difficult process of becoming strong, handsome and able men.

INTRODUCTION

People can be hard to understand sometimes, especially when you are on the autism spectrum (which includes Asperger syndrome). Sometimes people don't talk about the really important things in life. Sometimes they tell you not to talk about things in public and then you hear lots of people talking about the same thing in the school yard or on the radio. Sometimes people tell you different rules about the same thing. For example, your friend might say it is ok to smoke and your parents say it is not ok. It can be very confusing. But it is always good to know the facts. This book is full of important facts that people don't talk about all that much but are still really important. Knowing these facts will help you to be more prepared for some of the things that are going to happen to you in your teenage years.

Getting older brings lots of changes. Sometimes these changes can be difficult. It can be really confusing when your body starts changing, your friends suddenly start talking about girls or your mum wants you to take a shower *every day!* But when you know why things are changing and have some tactics to deal with them, change doesn't have to be so bad.

There are lots of great things about getting older. You get to stay up later at night, and do things and go to places you wouldn't have been able to as a child. Everybody

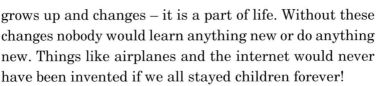

grows up and changes – it is a part of life. Without these changes nobody would learn anything new or do anything new. Things like airplanes and the internet would never have been invented if we all stayed children forever!

In this book you will learn all about your body and how it will change in the years ahead. You will learn about some of the great things about being a boy as well as the great things about being on the autism spectrum. You'll also learn about some of the new feelings you will have and get some tips on how to deal with them.

You will also read about puberty, which is a time when hormones (which are helpful chemicals in your body) start changing your body from a boy into a man.

Puberty starts for boys roughly between the ages of 11 and 17. During and after puberty there are all kinds of changes in your body, like getting more muscly and your skin getting oilier. However, these changes start at different times and change at different speeds for different boys. Your body will do what is right for you at its own pace. Some of the things in this book may have already started for you, and some may not.

After you have read this book, you might want some more information on some of the topics. You might have some questions. Believe me, even adults don't understand all of this stuff! It is a really good thing to ask people questions when you don't understand something.

Some of the things in this book are *private* topics. When something is private, it means you have to be careful about *who* you talk about it with and *where* you talk about it. Lots of things in this book should only be spoken about with your parents, other trusted adults and close friends. You can ask your parents or another trusted adult if you are unsure about who you can talk to about these things.

 BODIES

YOUR BODY IS AMAZING

Your body is amazing.

It helps you laugh and see and run and hear and feel and think and love all the great things in your life.

It is important to look after your body so that it can keep doing all of these things.

Looking after your body means doing regular exercise, sleeping well and eating healthy food (at least most of the time!).

It means not putting bad things into it, like smoke from cigarettes, alcohol or drugs.

Looking after your body also means going to the doctor or dentist when you need to.

It is a good idea to pay attention to what your body is 'telling you'.

Of course, your body doesn't actually talk to you!

What this means is when you feel tired, take a nap. If you feel hungry, eat something. And if you feel pain, tell someone so they can help you fix it!

REAL BODIES LOOK GREAT!

All bodies are different.

Some bodies are muscly. Some bodies are slim.

Some bodies are tall. Some bodies are short.

Lots of bodies are just in the middle.

All bodies are perfect in their own way.

Boys' bodies change when they start to become a man, usually between the ages of 11 and 17.

This time of life is called puberty.

During puberty your body will grow taller and wider.

You will grow hair in new places and the hair you have will get thicker.

Your penis and testicles may get bigger.

You will become more muscly.

Your body keeps changing throughout your life, but not as much or as quickly as it does during puberty.

Bodies in the real world aren't as perfect, muscly or slim as the ones you see on TV or in adverts.

It has taken a lot of make-up (yes, even on men!), special lighting and computer tricks for them to look like that.

Your real amazing body looks much better than any fake picture in a magazine.

HAIR

HAIR IN NEW PLACES

Both boys and girls grow hair in new places during puberty.

New hair can grow almost anywhere on your body!

One of the new places that boys grow hair is over their testicles.

This is called pubic hair.

Pubic hair is shorter, thicker and curlier than the hair on your head and can be a different colour.

Hair will also start to grow under your arms and on your chest.

More hair will grow on your arms and legs and it might become a bit darker and thicker than the hair already there.

You will also grow hair on your face around your mouth.

This hair growth will probably first start above your lips (this is called a 'moustache').

The hair on your face will probably look quite patchy at first, not like the older men you see who have full beards.

You might even grow hair on your back, hands and feet.

None of the hair on your body will grow long like the hair on your head.

Some boys grow lots of hair all over their bodies and some boys grow hardly any. Both of these are normal and look great!

SHAVING

Because it is patchy, when it first starts to grow you will probably need to shave off your moustache and the rest of the new hair on your face.

Learning to shave can be a bit tricky at first but it gets much easier with practice.

Most men shave about once a day (if they don't have a beard of course!).

Most teenagers shave about once a week.

When your hair grows back after shaving it feels a bit rough. This is called stubble.

You only need to shave again if you feel stubble on your face.

You can shave with electric razors or traditional razors.

Electric razors are easy to use and can't hurt you.

You need to be much more careful with traditional razors because they are dangerously sharp and more difficult to use.

To use traditional razors you will need to use foam and warm water on your face.

You will need an adult to teach you how to shave safely.

However, traditional razors do cut the hair shorter than electric razors so you might not need to shave as often.

After you shave, it is a good idea to put moisturising cream on your face so that your skin doesn't get dry and sore.

SQUEAK BOY STUFF SQUEAK

ALL ABOUT PENISES

Boys' and men's penises all look different.

Some are large, some are small.

Some are thick, some are thin.

Some boys have a slight bend to their penis.

Testicles also vary in shape and size.

Some men have one testicle bigger than the other.

All boys are born with what is called a 'foreskin', which is a bit of skin covering the top of their penis.

In some countries and religions, boys have their foreskins removed when they are babies.

This is called being circumcised.

Most of the time penises are floppy.

When they are erect, penises are much bigger and harder and stick out.

No matter how big or how small your penis is, most penises are about the same size when they are erect.

There is nothing you can do to make your penis bigger.

Tiny lumps and bumps on your penis and testicles are probably nothing to worry about.

But if you feel big lumps in your testicles, or you have lumps or bumps that hurt or are itchy, it is a good idea to get them checked out by a doctor.

VOICE CHANGES

Before puberty, boys' and girls' voices are similar.

During puberty things start to change and both their voices get lower.

Girls' voices only get a little bit lower.

The change is much more obvious for boys whose voices become *much* lower and they start sounding like a man.

This change is caused by hormones released during puberty making your larynx (your voice box) grow bigger.

Some boys experience a gradual and slow drop in their voice.

But for some boys the change happens very quickly.

The time of life when a boy's voice starts to change is called when his 'voice breaks'.

Don't worry, nothing actually breaks and it doesn't hurt at all!

But be prepared, during this time when you talk you might suddenly make unpredictable, high noises.

Some boys get embarrassed when this happens in front of other people.

But it happens to all boys and is totally normal.

These sudden high noises only last for a few seconds and they stop happening after a few months.

WHAT IS HAPPENING TO MY PENIS?

ERECTIONS

An erection is when your penis gets hard and points away from your body.

Some boys start getting erections at a young age. They are completely normal and happen to all boys and men.

During puberty, you will get a lot more erections, sometimes several times a day.

You might get an erection if you see something sexy or think sexy thoughts.

A lot of the time during puberty you can get an erection without any real reason. Sometimes you can get erections when you really don't want one!

This happens much less after puberty, when your body gets used to all the new hormones.

Most erections go away after a few minutes. There are some things that you can do to cover up erections that happen in public:

★ Sit down.

★ Cover your erection with a book or bag.

★ Make an excuse to leave the room.

★ Wear long shirts that cover your groin area.

★ Wear stiff trousers (such as jeans) which don't show up erections as much as loose fabrics.

★ Try to concentrate on 'unsexy' things.

WET DREAMS

Both girls and boys dream about sexy things sometimes.

Sometimes when boys dream about sexy things they get erections in their sleep.

Sometimes boys ejaculate in their sleep.

This means that semen comes out of their penis.

This is called a 'wet dream'.

Wet dreams happen to lots of boys, usually when they are going through puberty.

When you have a wet dream, your sheets and pyjamas will get wet with semen.

Semen is wet at first but then dries and stays in your sheets.

If you wake up with a wet patch near your penis during puberty, it is probably not pee but semen from a wet dream.

After a wet dream you will need to put the dirty pyjamas and sheets in the wash basket.

You will need to put clean sheets on your bed.

You will need to have a shower.

Wet dreams are a private topic.

It is only ok to talk about wet dreams with close and trusted friends, your mum or dad or another trusted adult.

HYGIENE

KEEPING YOUR BODY CLEAN

During puberty you start getting more oil all over your body.

This means that your hair and your body get dirtier and smellier much quicker.

Because of this you will need to start having a bath or shower every day.

Use soap or shower gel to help clean your body.

Make sure to wash the certain parts of your body that can get particularly smelly, like under your arms, your feet and your bottom.

Also make sure to clean your penis properly.

If you are not circumcised, this means very gently pulling back your foreskin and washing underneath it with warm water and soap or shower gel.

Wash your hair with shampoo and conditioner if you need it.

If you don't like the smell of certain soaps, shampoos or shower gels there are lots of different ones you can try.

There are also brands that have no perfume added.

If you find it difficult to remember all the steps to keeping clean, you could put a helpful checklist up somewhere near the shower.

OTHER IMPORTANT HYGIENE STUFF

There are other ways to help keep you looking and smelling clean besides washing.

During puberty you will also need to start wearing deodorant under your arms every day.

There are lots of different kinds of deodorant, like spray, roll-on or stick deodorants. You might need to try different deodorants before you find the right one.

You can buy deodorant that has no scent if you don't like the way any of them smell.

If you don't wash every day and wear deodorant, people will notice the smell and think that it is horrible.

It's important to brush and floss your teeth twice a day.

If your breath is smelly because you don't brush your teeth, people will start avoiding you to escape from the smell.

There are lots of different flavours of toothpaste you can try if you don't like the taste of mint.

Brushing your teeth also means that you won't have to go to the dentist as much in the future.

Mouthwash is another great way to keep your breath smelling nice, but it can have a very strong taste.

Keeping your fingernails and toenails cut short and kept clean is also important.

Remember that it is also important to wash your hands with warm water and soap after you have used the toilet or after you have touched your penis or bum.

 CLOTHES

CLEAN CLOTHES

As you get older, it becomes even more important to wear clean clothes.

People will not want to be close to you if your clothes are smelly and dirty.

Of course, accidents happen sometimes.

No need to worry if something spills on you during the day; just wipe it off as best you can.

If you are playing sports you don't need to worry about getting dirty at all – it is part of the fun.

But you should at least aim to leave your house in clean clothes!

It is also really important as you get older to learn to clean and dry your own clothes.

This can be a bit tricky at first but gets easier with practice.

Sometimes it is hard to know *when* your clothes need to be cleaned.

As a rule, underwear and socks should only be worn once before washing them.

Other clothes can be worn two to three times unless they are stained, smelly or dirty.

You can wear coats lots and lots of times before they need to be washed, unless they get stained.

THE RIGHT CLOTHES

It is important to wear the right clothes to the right place, like not wearing swimming trunks to school.

It is important to wear clothes that match the weather that day, like not wearing a raincoat when it is sunny.

It is important to wear clothes that fit you properly, like not wearing a t-shirt that is too small or tight.

It is good to have a rule that you always check your trouser zipper before you leave the toilet to make sure that it is zipped all the way up.

It's also not good if people can see your underwear over your trousers.

To help with all this stuff, some boys put a full-length mirror near their front door at home.

Before they leave the house each day they look in the mirror and check their clothes to make sure that everything is ok.

Some boys ask a trusted person for help.

But most importantly, you should wear clothes that you are comfortable in.

You will find it hard to concentrate on all the good stuff going on around you if you are wearing a scratchy fabric or your shoes are too tight!

SKIN

SPOTS

There are different types of spots called whiteheads and blackheads.

Spots can also look red or pink.

Spots can be big or small.

Some people get more spots than others.

Sometimes spots can hurt a little bit, but mostly they don't.

You can get spots on your face, but also on your chest and back or other parts of your body.

Boys and girls usually start getting spots around the time that puberty begins.

Spots are caused when all the oil that your body makes during puberty mixes with bacteria and dead skin cells on your skin.

This clogs up your pores (tiny holes in your skin that everyone has) and causes spots.

Everyone gets spots from time to time, even adults!

There are lots of things that you can do to help with spots, but nothing will get rid of all of them.

The most important thing to do is not to waste your time worrying about them.

Most of your spots will have cleared up all on their own by the end of your teenage years.

LOOKING AFTER YOUR SKIN

The most important thing you can do to prevent spots is to wash your face twice a day, especially at the end of the day.

Do this with clean, warm water and a special soap or facewash.

Clean your hands first before using them to wash your face.

Make sure to wash off all of the soap or facewash.

Then dry your face gently on a clean towel.

Apart from when you are washing it, avoid touching your face with your hands.

This can spread oil and make your face dirty (the kind of dirt that you can't see).

It is not a good idea to pick at or squeeze your spots.

This makes them even worse and can also cause scarring on your skin.

There are things you can buy in the chemist to help with spots.

But these will not get rid of *all* your spots.

There are also pills and creams that only a doctor can give you to help.

Looking after your skin also means wearing sunscreen or covering up when you are going to be out in the sun for a long time.

EMOTIONS

UNDERSTANDING EMOTIONS

People feel lots of different emotions, sometimes at the same time, like joyful, annoyed, excited, pleased, serious, sorry, hopeful, loving, careless or stressed.

Emotions are reactions to things that happen around you.

They are all connected to a reaction in your body.

When you are nervous, you might get what people call 'butterflies in your stomach'.

This doesn't really mean there are butterflies inside you, just that you have a fluttery feeling in your stomach.

People can blush when embarrassed, or cry when they are sad.

Crying is a normal reaction to strong emotions.

When people are afraid or angry, their heart can thump harder and faster and they might even sweat or feel dizzy.

It can often be hard to know *what* you are feeling and *why*.

Sometimes it can feel as if you are not in control of your feelings. But you are.

Negative feelings like sadness, anger or stress are normal and a part of life.

However, you should not be feeling them *all* of the time.

If you are feeling sad, angry or stressed a lot, there are lots of things that you can do to help.

LOOKING AFTER YOUR EMOTIONS

Here is a list of things you can do to help you look after your emotions:

* Don't hold them all inside! Tell people about your feelings by talking or writing notes. If you don't want to tell someone else, keep a Feelings Diary.

* Learn to take deep breaths. These are great to do if you are feeling stressed or angry. Take long slow breaths in through your nose and out through your mouth.

* Use your imagination. Think about places or things that make you feel relaxed.

* Exercise, eat well and get enough sleep.

* Think positive thoughts, like, 'I will try my best' and 'I can do this!' when you are about to do something you are nervous about.

* Spend time with people who make you feel good.

* Face your fears. It is a good thing sometimes to do things we find a bit scary (like going to a party). This way, we learn that the thing wasn't so bad after all and it will be a bit less scary the next time.

* Make a list every day of things you are grateful for. You can think of the list in your head if you don't want to write it down. Your list could include having a cool bedroom, a kind dad, a granny who buys you comics, a day off school or a new game. Anything that makes you happy that day!

♡♡ CRUSHES ♡♡

UNDERSTANDING CRUSHES

Having a crush means that you like someone in a romantic way.

When you have a crush you might want to be near that person *a lot*.

You might think about them *a lot*.

You might feel excited and have problems concentrating, especially when the person you like is around!

You might even feel those pretend butterflies in your stomach you read about earlier.

You might want to touch them or kiss them, or have them touch or kiss you.

Lots of boys and girls get crushes on each other from a young age.

But little crushes can become big crushes during and after puberty.

Boys can have crushes on someone in school, a friend, an actress or actor, a teacher or a friend's big sister.

They are a normal part of growing up.

Boys start having crushes on people at different ages.

You might have crushes on certain people or you might not be interested yet. Both are ok.

WHAT TO DO IF YOU HAVE A CRUSH ON SOMEONE

If you have a crush on someone famous or much older or younger than you, you can think about them and talk to trusted people about them.

But it is not a good idea to try to have a romantic relationship with them.

Acting on a crush with someone much younger or much older than yourself can get you into serious trouble.

If you have a crush on someone around your own age, it is a good idea to start off by being friends.

This might mean talking to them about things they like, or doing something fun together.

It is not a good idea to follow them or stare at them. They will think that is weird.

Answer these questions about the person you have a crush on:

★ Do they make you feel good about yourself?

★ Do they try to spend time with you?

★ Do they include you in games?

★ Do they say nice things to you?

If they are not doing any of these things, it might be better not to waste any more time having a crush on them.

You can't make someone like you.

Liking someone who also likes you back feels so much nicer.

⚾ FRIENDS ⚾

UNDERSTANDING FRIENDSHIP

A friend is someone you like to spend time with who also likes to spend time with you.

You don't need to have lots of friends, but it is good to have at least one good friend.

Not everyone will want to be your friend. This is ok.

Friends care about each other and are kind to each other.

Friends help you when you have a problem.

They help you feel good about yourself.

If someone makes you feel bad, they are not your friend.

Friends share their feelings with each other.

Just because a friend disagrees with you about something, it doesn't mean that you can't still be friends.

Disagreeing is part of being human!

Friends aren't perfect. They can make mistakes sometimes.

Sometimes friendships change. Sometimes friendships end.

It is sad when someone does not want to be your friend any more.

This happens to everybody.

It does not mean that there is something wrong with you.

It just means that it is time to look for a new friend.

MAKING AND KEEPING FRIENDS

It is good to think about how a friend should treat you.

Just because you *really* want a friend, it is not a good idea to be friends with someone who makes you feel bad.

You should also think about how *you* can be a good friend to other people.

This might mean listening to them when they are sad, sending them a birthday card on their birthday or going to a movie that they want to see, even if you don't really want to see it.

Being a good friend also means saying sorry when you have done something to hurt them – even if you really think that you were right!

Lots of people make friends when they are doing something they already enjoy, like playing football or playing in a chess club.

This means that they have lots in common and talking to each other is easier.

But sometimes even really good friends have no interests in common – they just like being together.

There is no magic formula to friendship!

 THE INTERNET

THE INTERNET CAN BE GREAT

The internet is amazing.

Much better than in the old days when people had to go all the way to the library for information they needed!

You can meet and chat with people online with the same interests as you, even if nobody else in your school or family shares this interest.

If you have difficulty with eye contact and body language it can be easier to 'chat' to someone by typing.

Online, you can create amazing things, like art, movies and music.

You can then share these with other people and see what they have created.

You can read about (or chat with) other children and teenagers on the autism spectrum who may be going through the same kinds of things as you.

Or you could find out tips for dealing with things you might find difficult, like writing essays.

If you are good with computers, there are also lots of different types of computer jobs that you might be good at and enjoy when you are a grown up.

THE INTERNET CAN BE DANGEROUS

Sometimes people online are not who they pretend to be.

Sometimes bad adults even pretend to be children.

Some websites are run by people who believe bad things and want other people to believe those things too.

Criminals use the internet to find out about someone so that they can rob them.

Not all of the information you read online is true.

Also, *nothing* on the internet is private.

A private email can end up being shared with hundreds of people by the next day.

If something online makes you uncomfortable, tell a trusted adult.

If you get a message that worries you, don't reply to it.

Don't post things like your name, birthday or phone number.

Never post pictures or videos of any part of your body, even to friends.

Don't arrange to meet someone without bringing along a trusted adult.

Ignore any message asking you for help or personal information, even if they say you have won something.

It is always a lie.

☆☆ YOUR BODY BELONGS TO YOU ☆☆

KNOWING YOUR BODY RIGHTS

Even though you are officially a child, you have rights.

Your body belongs to you!

Touch can feel nice.

However, someone should have a good reason for wanting to touch your body.

You don't have to touch someone else's body if you don't want to.

Other people can touch you only if you are happy for them to do so.

Touch should make you feel good.

Touch should not make you feel uncomfortable, or give you an 'uh oh' feeling inside.

Touch should not hurt, or make it hard for you to breathe.

You should never be asked to keep touch a secret.

Tickling can be ok but only if you like it (lots of people don't).

Doctors sometimes need to touch you for medical reasons.

Sometimes this can hurt but is it still ok touch because there is a very good reason for it. However, it is still a good idea to tell a doctor if what they are doing is hurting you.

Just because you like someone, it doesn't mean that they are allowed to touch you if you don't want them to.

HOW TO SAY 'NO!'

If you are not happy with the way someone is touching you, it is important to let them know that you are strong and that you know your body rights.

This is how you can do this:

* Stand with your feet firmly apart on the ground.

* Try to look the person in the eye.

* Put your arm out towards them, palm up to their face.

* Make sure that there is a serious expression on your face.

* Say 'No!' loudly and firmly.

Saying 'No!' in this way lets the person know that you are *very* serious.

If they keep bothering you, run away and tell someone you trust about what happened.

If that person does nothing about it, tell another person that you trust.

Even if they stop bothering you when you say 'No!' it is important to tell someone.

There is no need to say 'No!' in this way for every kind of touch, for example if your mum holds your arm when crossing the road.

Ask your parents or another trusted adult to help you learn the right times to say 'No!' in this way.

It's a good idea to practise saying 'No!' like this in the mirror and with trusted people.

I AM ME. ALL I EVER NEED TO BE

EVERYBODY IN THIS WORLD IS DIFFERENT AND UNIQUE

People like different things.

People think different things are important.

Some people think it is important to get good grades in school, while other people think it is more important to do well in sports or look cool.

People even feel different emotions about exactly the same things.

For example, some people love birds and other people are afraid of them.

People see and hear the world around them differently.

Some people don't even notice bright lights while others can't think properly because it hurts their eyes if there is a bright light in the room.

Some people like having lots of friends and others prefer to have just one friend.

Some people like being around other people all the time and others really need some alone time during the day.

Some people really want to get married and have children, and others aren't that bothered.

Everyone has things that they are good at and things they find difficult.

The world would be a very boring place if everyone felt, acted and thought the same!

KNOWING AND LOVING *YOU*

If you are reading this book, you probably have this thing called autism (or Asperger syndrome).

This means you think a little bit differently from most people.

Not worse. Just different.

And there are lots and lots and lots of other people who think just like you!

There are so many great things about being on the autism spectrum, like being honest, reliable, good at thinking logically and having a strong sense of what is right and what is wrong.

You are probably good at concentrating on one thing for a long time.

You also probably know loads of information about some things.

You might find it difficult to talk to people in a crowd, or understand why people do certain things.

But that's ok.

There are lots and lots of people who can't do the things you do easily.

Be proud of the amazing person that you are.

You don't have to be the same as everyone else.

All you have to be is the best version of you.

 SO WHAT ABOUT GIRLS?

Girls also go through puberty, but it starts a little bit earlier than boys. Some of the changes that happen to girls are the same as boys, and some are very different:

* Girls also get oilier skin.

* They also get smellier more quickly.

* They grow more hair (much less than you!) and in new places.

* They also have to deal with spots.

* They grow breasts.

* Their hips get a bit wider.

* They get crushes too.

* They start periods (which is when a small amount of blood comes out of their vaginas for a few days, once a month).

* They do not have to deal with their voice 'breaking'.

* They don't have penises so don't have to deal with things like unexpected erections or wet dreams.

Girls think that all of this stuff is just as confusing as you do!

ADVICE FOR PARENTS AND PROFESSIONALS

What is this book about?

This book is written for pre-teen and teenage boys on the autism spectrum. It is formatted and written to work towards their specific learning strengths, in that it is highly visual, with written language kept visually uncluttered, concrete and clear.

The aim of the book is to provide a starting point for boys on the spectrum to learn about the physical, sensory, social and emotional aspects of puberty, including hair growth, erections, body image, hygiene, spots, friendship, crushes, emotions and understanding and loving themselves both as an individual and as an individual on the autism spectrum. Practical tips are provided in each of these areas, specifically addressing issues commonly raised by men on the spectrum, for example sensory issues affecting shaving, and addressing euphemisms or figures of speech in areas that can cause confusion (e.g. 'voices breaking').

Beyond matters related to puberty, the book also encompasses other important issues of safety relevant to teenagers today, including saying 'No' to unwanted touch and keeping safe while enjoying the internet.

Why do young people on the autism spectrum need this book?

Most children learn (often confusing and contradictory) information about growing up from many different places, including friends, family, books and TV. Children with autism can miss a lot of this information, and the information they do take on they find even more difficult to decode. Because of this, they need explicit teaching in what may seem obvious to other people – in other words the 'hidden curriculum' of life (for example, that it's not ok to follow someone around all day if you have a crush on them).

Although they may be delayed in some areas of development, children on the spectrum will experience puberty, adolescence and all that goes with that at the same time as everyone else. However, they have to deal with these through a prism of autism, which includes core difficulties with change itself. Add in difficulties arising from the triad of impairments (social skills, language and restricted and repetitive behaviours) and fewer opportunities to learn from other children, and there is the potential for a number of issues if they are not given adequate preparation, information and support.

In addition, children on the spectrum can be vulnerable because of difficulties interpreting the motives of others, a desire to be accepted socially, uncertainty about what a real friendship constitutes and difficulties reporting past events. It is a parent's natural instinct to protect their children. However, avoiding topics such as private body parts can teach a child that they are either unimportant or shameful and are not to be spoken about. Overprotection from information about sexuality, bodies, safety awareness and healthy and unhealthy relationships leaves children vulnerable. Also remember that every skill you teach a child to do independently makes them less reliant on other people to support them in adulthood. This has important safety implications for those tasks that involve privacy and sexual body parts, such as changing your pyjamas and sheets after a wet dream, showering and looking after your sexual health.

Adolescence is also a time when children can become acutely aware of their differences and how they affect their lives. Developing a healthy and realistic identity (one of the hallmarks of adolescence) means understanding your own personal weaknesses as well as your strengths. Children on the spectrum need to learn about their diagnosis, the challenges that come with this diagnosis, what they need to overcome these challenges, and how to go about getting them (for example, being able to tell their teacher, 'I find it difficult to listen to you when that light is flickering. Can we please turn it off?'). This book supports this understanding in a positive and respectful manner.

When is the right time to give a young person this book?
Remember that people on the spectrum can struggle with even small changes in their lives. Learning in general can also be slow and confusing,

especially if it is anything to do with the social realm. Trying to teach things like good hygiene during puberty, already a turbulent time, can cause unnecessary confusion. Better to start as soon as possible, giving information that is appropriate to their age and developmental level.

How do I use this book?
This book can be used in a number of ways. It can be given to a young person to read independently if you feel that they have the motivation and language ability to do so. You may also choose to read it with them, adapting the level of language to their personal language needs. Topics do not need to be read sequentially and can be used as and when needed. It will be important, however, that it is re-read a number of times to support retention of information.

After reading the book with a young person, it would be a good idea to ask them whether they have any questions about it or if there were any bits that they found confusing or didn't understand. Their answers can be the starting point of further work in this area.

What else can I do?
This book just skims the surface of all there is to know about these topics in what will be a lifelong learning process. Let's face it, most adults find this stuff confusing a lot of the time. It should therefore be seen as a starting point, a conversation starter, for more advanced learning in the specific areas where a young person will need support.

Be careful to provide the information to them in a way that they understand. This might mean reducing language, focusing on pictures and single words, adding speech or thought bubbles to comic-type graphics or delving into more complex topics of intimate relationships with longer pieces of text.

Remember to give the information clearly and calmly. Use a positive tone and don't overload the young person with information or language. Be concrete and use correct terminology (i.e. not made-up names that nobody outside the child's family will understand). Teach young people with good language skills the correct words to use when talking to teachers or other adults, but also the words that are ok to use with their peers when there are no adults around. Be careful about language being taken literally (for example, boys' voices do not literally 'break').

Given that this book is aimed at a pre-teen developmental level there are a lot of other topics, such as consent and contraception, that are important for older teenagers and young adults to learn about. However, even for pre-teens, it would be a good idea to create a scrapbook or folder for all those further areas that aren't covered in this book, and to address topics which are included but in more detail. This could be added to and adapted as the young person gets older and becomes ready for more advanced topics and would have the added benefit of containing pictures and relevant information that might help their understanding, for example pictures of members of their family growing from a baby into an adult.

Another very important thing to do is to talk to the young person about their diagnosis and what it means for them. This does not have to be done in one big difficult conversation. Start talking about difference early. Normalise disability. Read books about autism with them geared for their age and ability level. Research the Autistic Self Advocacy Network. Introduce them (through books, TV or the internet) to role models who have a disability. One of the best things that you can do to develop your own understanding of autism is to read books by authors on the spectrum – they have a lot to teach us.

Another important thing to do is to provide real-life practice in some of these areas, for example role plays or supported experiences in the community. People on the autism spectrum can be very good at learning by rote what they should do in a certain situation (for example, being able to list internet safety rules), but can have difficulty applying this knowledge when it matters. Real-life practice is vital, as is repetition.

FURTHER READING

For young people

Robbie Harris writes excellent, colour illustrated books published by Candlewick Publishers in the area of sex education for typically developing children of various ages. These books can be used for the illustrations alone if the level of language used is an issue.

- *It's So Amazing: A Book about Eggs, Sperm, Birth, Babies and Families* (ages seven and over) (2004).

- *It's Perfectly Normal: Changing Bodies, Growing Up, Sex and Sexual Health* (ages ten and over) (2009).

For parents and professionals

See Jessica Kingsley Publishers' website for a wide range of autism-specific books for parents, professionals and children (www.jkp.com).

My website Autism Sex Education (www.autismsexeducation.com) provides a comprehensive list of relevant resources, books and multimedia sources.

Professionals looking for advice on how to provide an evidence-supported, comprehensive, individualised and developmentally appropriate sexuality and relationship education programme to students that they work with (of which this book can be seen as an accompanying resource) should access my book *Sexuality and Relationship Education for Children and Adolescents with Autism Spectrum Disorder: A Professional's Guide to Understanding, Preventing Issues, Supporting Sexuality and Responding to Inappropriate Behaviours*, published by Jessica Kingsley Publishers (2014).